THE IMPORTANCE OF PARENT-TEACHER COLLABORATION FOR CHILDREN'S SUCCESS

THE IMPORTANCE OF PARENT-TEACHER COLLABORATION FOR CHILDREN'S SUCCESS

AVERY NIGHTINGALE

Creative Quill Press

CONTENTS

1 Introduction   1
2 Benefits of Parent-Teacher Partnership   2
3 Strategies for Effective Collaboration   9
4 Overcoming Challenges in Parent-Teacher Partnership   15
5 Promoting Parent Engagement and Involvement   21
6 Conclusion   27

Copyright © 2024 by Avery Nightingale

All rights reserved. No part of this book may be reproduced in any manner whatsoever without written permission except in the case of brief quotations embodied in critical articles and reviews.

First Printing, 2024

CHAPTER 1

Introduction

As we look to the future where our children will be the leaders of tomorrow, we ask what we can do to ensure their success for a future that is unclear. It is an unsettling feeling for anyone who takes on the responsibility of shaping these children to adulthood, whether they are parents, teachers or the community. It has become evident that a child's academic success is directly related to their academic achievement. Parental involvement and work to support their child has been proven to be integral in a child's success. Although it has been standard for a parent to be involved in the earlier years of a child's education, it is not quite the same today. Today, children have a higher workload, more is expected of them and the curriculum is more complex. In fact, with each new grade level, a child's success rate can be determined by a new set of standards. This makes it essential for a parent to understand what is expected of the child at each grade level and communicate the same expectations to the teacher. This way, the parent and teacher can work together to ensure the child's success at that level.

CHAPTER 2

Benefits of Parent-Teacher Partnership

Parent's active involvement in their children's learning is key to their children's success not just in school, but throughout their lives. The role of parent's involvement in children's school lives has shifted dramatically in the last fifty years. In the past, parent involvement was often limited to helping with homework, volunteering in the school, and attending parent-teacher conferences. Today, many parents take an active role in their children's education, participating in a variety of formal and informal activities to support their children's learning at home and at school. Teachers who seek to involve parents as partners in education will find that they can build their awareness of children's cognitive abilities and how to develop them, foster a classroom environment that is conducive to learning, and work with parents to support their children's learning at home. As a result of this teacher-parent partnership, there is a greater likelihood that the benefits of parent involvement will extend to the home. When parents and teachers work as partners in a child's education, there is an increased likelihood that a child will perform better in school. This is due to a collective effort between parents and teachers to understand the child's abilities and plan a course of action that will help the child reach his or her full potential. Through learning about what is taught at school, parents can gain a better understanding of their child's strengths and weaknesses and help their child with targeted support. For example, if a teacher has informed a parent that their child is struggling with reading, the parent can work with the teacher to find out what the child is finding difficult and learn what strategies the teacher is using to improve the child's reading skills. With this knowledge, the parent can attempt to supplement what the child is learning at school with additional teaching at home. This might involve reading to the child more often, finding books and resources that are at the right level for the child, or practicing specific skills recommended by the teacher. By taking this targeted approach, there is a greater likelihood that parents' work will support what the teacher is doing and have a positive impact on the child's learning.

Improved Academic Performance

Teachers are seen as academic guides for students but in the end, the primary source of learning for a student is their home environment. It is widely known that students imitate their parents' behavior. Because of this, if a parent expresses a keen interest in education and shows a positive learning attitude, the student will mimic this behavior. The strong parent-teacher relationship creates a positive learning environment for a student as there is consistency with teacher attitudes towards learning and the attitudes and behavior that a student will witness from their parents. In such cases where parents are fully involved in the academic life of their child, teachers have constantly praised the change in student behavior and work ethics. In parent-teacher interviews, as one teacher indicated, there has been a clear change in student attitudes towards learning for the better. The student spends more time completing tasks and shows increased class participation; the change has been a noticeable one.

The core purpose of schooling is to enhance the academic acumen of students. Parents and teachers need to work together to enable students to perform to their true potential. This means that teachers should have the opportunity to converse with parents to discuss the learning style and capabilities of a student both inside and outside of the classroom. Only then will teachers be able to tailor specific teaching methodologies and strategies to the student and better assist in a student's learning. It will also give teachers a better understanding as to why students may be underperforming and what they can potentially do to assist. With the extra knowledge provided by parents, teachers can potentially open up new learning windows for an individual student. The result of this will be a more effective education experience for a student and consequently enhanced performance.

Enhanced Social and Emotional Development

Expanded social and emotional development Alluding to guardians truly helping out and being a piece of the school, understudies will get the feeling that what they do is significant. This will pass on an amazing message and help them to feel more like a piece of a network. With expanded parent contribution in training, kids frequently feel more emotionally and socially secure. At the point when guardians partake in instruction, kids regularly build up better relational abilities and improved conduct – the two constructs that emphatically affect confidence. Get familiar with how to enable your youngster to create Social and Emotional Learning (SEL) abilities from home, a joint venture between the National PTA and the Association for Supervision and Curriculum Development (ASCD). Social and enthusiastic turn of events (nurture) is a field of formative brain science that is about a kid's developing mind—the way that job and the development of outline of living things from time to time or rapidly develops and changes over the long run. Measures changed as expected, alluded to size or degree of things, are found in a child's plentiful response vacillate and development of trial. Successful turn of events and learning, including SEL, depends on a comprehension of the complex associations among science, brain research, and instructive practice.

Increased Motivation and Engagement

Numerous studies have concluded that student motivation in schools can be an important factor in socio-emotional and academic development, and various intervention strategies have been developed to increase motivation. The role of parents in children's academic and social development has been a focus of research, with the general belief that parental involvement has a positive influence on student motivation. Some longitudinal studies have shown that parents' aspirations and beliefs for their child's future success can be a strong predictor of that child's motivation and achievement. Teachers may often echo a parent's influence, and when both parents and teachers have high aspirations for a student, the student tends to be more positively motivated. Parental aspiration also influences students' own aspirations for their futures, which in turn predicts student motivation and achievement. Since parents' influence is greatest in the earliest years of a child's education, it is important for them to foster a positive attitude and strong self-belief in their children, as well as the belief that effort leads to success. Positive attitudes and beliefs concerning achievement are significant predictors of motivation and learning. A study on academic socialization found that children model their parents' behaviors; if parents demonstrate that they value education and are involved in home support activities, children are more likely to adopt achieving orientations towards their own education. Given the significant impact of parental influence, it would be hasty to dismiss a partnership that has the potential to increase parents' involvement in a major context that affects students' motivation.

Better Behavior and Discipline

Parent involvement and collaboration are key components in a child's learning process and behavior. Students whose parents are involved in their schooling have more positive attitudes and behavior in comparison to those whose parents are not involved. When parents are involved in their children's education, children are more likely to be self-disciplined, polite, and cooperative. It showed that the more parental involvement in education, the lower the chances were for their children to receive suspension. Students with the most consistent parental involvement, regardless of race, gender, family income, or education, have the highest grades and test scores, as well as better social skills and behavior. This information conveys that it is not only important for children to behave and have better self-control, but also to have consistent parental involvement and collaboration in their education. This information is relevant to my research essay showing that parents and teachers need to collaborate for success in the child's academics and behavior. Both parents and teachers need to communicate with each other to address the child's behavior and work out action plans to help the child improve on their behavior. An example of parent and teacher collaboration in helping a student with behavior is by communicating and forming an action plan to help the student improve on their organizational skills and become more self-disciplined. The teacher could assign daily planner checks for the student to record down homework deadlines and test dates as well as making up a reward system to positively reinforce the student when they demonstrate good behavior and follow through with their planner checks. The parents would also be encouraged to always communicate and stay updated with the child's teacher to ensure that they are following through with the action plan. This constructive program was able to help a 12-year-old ADHD student gain more self-discipline and organizational skills in and out of the classroom. This example demonstrates various ways that teachers and parents can work together to help children improve on their behavior.

Strengthened Home-School Connection

For ELLs, meaningful parental engagement is more significant to assist positive education, whether it be learning English or academic content. When this situation is applied to most Southeast Asian countries, the English education support from parents might be in the form of initiation to communicate with the school and/or program to improve children's English language learning at home, with the hope that they can assist their children in case of anything. In this case, the school might develop a certain program, for example, "English Corners in Each Home," to create efficient learning for ELLs.

Home-school partnership brings a high propensity to enable children's success at school. Thus, one of the important shifts to develop is to create a strong attachment between schools, families, and communities. Epstein argued that the most effective types of parent involvement are those which engage parents in working directly with their children on learning activities at home. These activities send a positive confirmation that the children's learning is important and the school values family support for their children's learning. According to Dauber & Epstein, families are integral parts of the "teaching team" when the families can assist their children's learning at home and express high aspirations for their children's achievement. Schlomer also reasoned that a supportive family plays a role in fulfilling children's needs and motivation toward accomplishment in school. Children from supportive families are more confident in their academic claiming that there is strong support from parents believing that they are doing good or can improve in school.

CHAPTER 3

Strategies for Effective Collaboration

Open, two-way communication is imperative. Always encourage parents to express their concerns and ask questions regarding their child's education. Most parents will be able to share some aspect of the child's behavior or school experiences that will help you better understand his/her performance. Understanding different cultural communication norms is also something the teacher may need to consider. For example, some cultures may express dissatisfaction or concerns in their child's education if they feel the child has not met their expectations academically. It would be expected that the teacher would take some form of corrective action in response. On the other hand, lack of engagement may be a sign of trust in the teacher's professional expertise and a belief that the child will be guided in the right direction. Meeting face to face is the preferred mode of communication but it is not always possible. In some cases, non-English speaking parents may feel uncomfortable speaking with a teacher in person. Utilizing an interpreter over the phone may be the best option in such cases. Written communication via diaries or email is also an effective way for parents to communicate with the teacher. Teachers can use diary writing to provide feedback regarding a child's progress and written information can be spread to all parents in multicultural classrooms. Email is great for sending longer, more detailed messages and attachments, particularly in secondary education where student roll may be in excess of 150 students. Teachers can share the results from assessment activities and the relevant marking rubrics with parents so they have a clear understanding of their child's progress and what is expected in future tasks.

Open and Transparent Communication

The primary means of fostering shared responsibility is through open and transparent communication. When parents and teachers are open and share their ideas and information, the potential for children's success is maximized. Some primary ways to enhance open and transparent communication is for the teacher to inform the parents on how they will recognize and reward their children for academic and social successes. Research has shown that the best feedback is contingent, immediate, specific, and positive. Such feedback has a strong influence on increasing children's self-esteem and motivation. Thus, it is important that parents and teachers regularly communicate so that the teacher can report instances where they have rewarded the child, and the parent can support the teacher's positive reinforcement. Information should flow from both the teacher and the parent. If the parent is to understand how to better assist their child with his/her homework, the teacher should be able to provide alternative ways of teaching concepts and be informed on what the child is struggling with. The amount of information that a teacher can provide a parent varies depending on the child's age and the type of task the child is learning. If a child is struggling with a particular mathematics concept, there may be instances where the teacher will need to explain the concept to the parent. This is referred to as the mediating effect and can involve more knowledgeable others teaching parents how to assist their children so that they, in turn, can help the parents truly understand the best way to help their children.

Regular Parent-Teacher Meetings

Meetings are also a chance for parents and teachers to discuss any issues or concerns that may be affecting the child and to identify the most suitable course of action. It is suggested by Hoover-Dempsey and Sandler (1997) that when parents and teachers are able to engage in activities that directly benefit their children, this is when parents feel most empowered and motivated to become involved. Regular meetings can lead to a sense of ownership of schooling by parents and a feeling that they are making valued contributions to decision making.

Meetings can be used for a broad range of purposes. A study by Hoover-Dempsey and Sandler (1997) identified four types of parent involvement behavior, with one of these being "discussion with parents about school-related issues". The authors found this to be the most effective method of involvement for student achievement. This highlights how regular parent-teacher meetings can facilitate parents supporting their children's learning at home and can lead to increased student motivation. By discussing their children's progress and actions that can be taken to assist further development, parents can form a clearer understanding of what is occurring in the classroom and what is expected of their children. This can lead to an increase in the quality and quantity of assistance parents provide at home.

Regular parent-teacher meetings are viewed as an essential tool for developing effective collaboration between home and school. They represent a time and place where two-way information sharing can occur and where the development of one-to-one personal relationships can take place. As suggested by Swap (1993), the formality of such meetings represents a tangible commitment by both parents and teachers to the process of working together.

Sharing Information and Resources

While the most common tools for sharing information between home and school are notes, memos, phone calls, and parent-teacher meetings, teachers should also find it useful to involve the parents in their child's education in more substantive ways. Teachers can provide parents with books, guides, and other materials on the subject of children's education, and then discuss with the parents their perceptions of these resources and ways they might be useful in understanding and teaching their children. Teachers might also introduce parents to useful assessment tools and data that are typically only available to the teachers themselves. For example, a teacher might video record a child in various school situations in order to demonstrate to the parents the child's behavior in their absence, and discuss with the parents the child's demeanor and how it might be read.

When it comes to sharing information and resources with parents, teachers have at their disposal a variety of tools and mechanisms. Sharing information is more than itemizing a child's behavior or academic progress; it is ensuring the parents' comprehension of that information and its implications. For example, while a teacher might know that the child's increased aggressiveness on the playground is due to being slighted by his friends, the parent may misinterpret that information as a sign of the teacher's inability to control the class. Teachers can head off such misunderstandings by ensuring that their communications are focused on the issues of concern and their interpretations.

Setting and Monitoring Goals

After goals have been set, an action plan should be etched outlining how they are to be achieved and who is responsible for specific tasks. For example, "Kevin's parents will read a book to him in Spanish twice a week to increase bilingual literacy". The teacher can also help students and parents make decisions about what students should do in order to make progress toward reaching their goals, and what help or resources should be provided. Goal-related activity and effort can then be monitored and assessed regularly, with student development and goal optimality informing the need for any goal adjustment. A unique aspect of the teacher-student collaboration is that students can play a direct and reflective role in the goal setting and assessment process aimed at self-regulation. These cognitive and metacognitive self-regulatory skills can provide social and emotional benefits to students and improve their learning outcomes.

Setting specific, achievable, and realistic goals is said to be the first step in successfully reaching any desired outcome. A successful student-teacher collaboration can be greatly enhanced by setting specific goals that are explicitly stated, feasible, and congruent with the students' needs and learning style. Goals can be set in the academic, behavioral, social, or self-regulatory realms. For example, "Joey will raise his hand and contribute to classroom discussion in all subject areas", "Maria will complete homework without help from her parents". Goal setting rates of self-efficacy and intrinsic interest in a student. A recent review of the literature involving teacher-set proximal goals or "just right" goals has also shown that students' and teachers' perceptions converge most when lessening the discrepancy between the students' goal and the teacher's goal for them.

Involving Parents in School Activities

Gathering information on the views of both teachers and parents as to the types of activities that should be undertaken can be productive. It is important that the activity is well-structured and the roles of parents and teachers are defined to avoid any embarrassing situations. Teachers who are coordinating the activities need to have good interpersonal skills and the ability to lead and manage groups. Activities should be started on a small scale if they are to be implemented for the first time. An effective approach is to target certain groups of parents rather than the whole school. If managed well, school activities can bring immense satisfaction to both parents and teachers and lead to improved parent-teacher relations.

This is an important strategy in improving the relationship between the parents and the school. Parents who are involved in school activities get to know the teachers and staff members better. It provides them with opportunities to communicate with the teachers informally and to understand what goes on in the school. There are many school activities which parents can be involved in, from fund raising, school discos, sports days, parent and child learning sessions, to more formal parent education programs. Involving parents in school activities can be a two-edged sword, as some parents may feel that the school is encroaching on their territory!

CHAPTER 4

Overcoming Challenges in Parent-Teacher Partnership

Another frequent barrier to parent-teacher partnership collaboration is conflicting expectations and priorities for parents and teachers. This can be linked in part to the nature of differing goals for students. Teachers often define success in terms of academic achievement, while parents may define success in broader terms, encompassing personal and social development as well as academic development. Discussing and reconciling these differing views is important, as it will allow parents and teachers to mutually work towards common goals for their students. An essential step in creating a solution to this issue is for teachers to attempt to understand what parents' priorities are, and to learn what they expect from their child's school. This can be done through direct communication with parents. Similarly, teachers can convey their expectations and goals for the class and for each individual student to the parents. This can be in the form of a newsletter, a note, or an informal conversation with parents.

Although the advantages of parent-teacher partnerships are clear and abundant, research findings convey that educators and parents often encounter difficulties in making this partnership collaborate to be beneficial for children. Quite possibly the most frequently cited barrier is the existence of language and cultural differences between teachers and families. It is a fact that the more an individual feels connected to a social entity, and the more the information is presented in a style or format that is familiar, the more likely the individual will feel positively about the social entity. Thus, when teachers are unable to communicate effectively with parents, they are less likely to involve those parents in the educational process. As a result, the student's achievement is likely to suffer, over and above the direct effect of the teacher's socio-economic status.

Language and Cultural Barriers

Teachers and parents may come from diverse cultural groups, leading to miscommunication and misunderstandings. If the teacher and parents do not speak the same language at home, the child may be required to translate, taking on a role that can create stress in some children. Mispronunciations of words and accents can cause native English-speaking teachers to lower expectations for non-native English-speaking parents. Knowledge of cultural differences helps explain varying perceptions and expectations. American parents may expect to be in charge of their children's education, while Asian parents may not only defer to the teacher's judgment but feel uncomfortable when asked to participate in their child's schooling. In American culture, it is the norm to question and even challenge the teacher's judgment. Teachers generally expect parents to participate in school events, help out with homework, limit TV watching, reading with their child, and to discuss and show interest in what their child is learning at school. Inner-city parents may have different expectations of the school and their children. They may only expect teachers to call when their child is misbehaving and limit their involvement in schooling. Creating meaningful parent participation starts with understanding and respecting the values and belief systems of the families involved. The teacher should create an inviting atmosphere and clearly communicate their goals for parent involvement, which may need to be tailored for different families. Learning should be inclusive of all family goals for their child and not dismissive of some expectations as unhelpful.

Conflicting Expectations and Priorities

To avoid or resolve conflicts, there must be effective communication of each parent or teacher's expectations and priorities. Open discussions should be encouraged, with each party making an effort to listen to the other's views. This will help to build a shared understanding of the child's needs, and will ensure that everyone is 'reading from the same page' in support of the child. It may be helpful to set specific, achievable goals for the child based on these discussions, so that progress can later be evaluated. The most prevalent setting for parent-teacher discussions of this nature is the parent-teacher interview. Unfortunately, this setting can be intimidating for parents and may not allow adequate time for discussion of all issues. An alternative approach is regular, informal contact between teacher and parent, be it through face-to-face conversation at the classroom door, email or phone. This approach may help parents to feel more comfortable and equal in their relationship with the teacher, and may provide a more accurate reflection of the teacher-parent dynamic as it directly involves the child's presence at home.

Parent-teacher collaboration can sometimes be complicated by conflicting expectations and priorities. Parents could expect the teacher to solve behavioral problems, while the teacher is likely to see the solution in terms of a joint parent-teacher approach. Alternatively, a teacher may try to promote a talent or skill which a parent deems unimportant in comparison to a focus on core subjects. Parents may also feel that the teacher expects them to replicate the school's activities at home. For instance, a study on parental involvement in homework from a Canadian inner-city school showed that parents of low socio-economic status felt that teachers expected them to provide substantial homework assistance, while teachers felt it was sufficient to simply ensure the student had a quiet place to work. All these scenarios can lead to a lack of follow-through by one or both of the parents, giving the impression to the teacher that the parents do not care about their child's education. Being aware of these potential disparities provides an opportunity for both parents and teachers to align their expectations and priorities for the benefit of the child.

Limited Time and Availability

Another method to improve time availability is to create scheduled regular meetings between parents and teachers. In an action-research project conducted by Simon, an elementary teacher, and his colleague Crespo, the pair found that the main reasons parents took little interest in the school were lack of interaction from the teacher and parents being unsure what they could offer in the way of helping their children. This program's main goal was to initiate a strong partnership between parents and teachers to support student learning. A vital aspect was that teachers were to schedule a minimum of two meetings with the parent(s) of each child. The results were excellent. The parents were open to scheduling meetings at various times and became more aware of the teacher's consideration towards making time to involve them in the child's education. The product of this was better parent insight in understanding assigned tasks, increased communication in parent inquiries, and an increase in monitoring student homework and assignments.

Parental time is of limited availability for many different reasons, such as work schedules, single parents running a household, and parents studying after work. A parent's time is spread thin, and often there is little time to spare. Teachers suggest that in order to break through this barrier, they need to gain an understanding of the family's situation. Teachers have to be sympathetic towards the parents, understanding that they too are under pressure and sometimes their own interest may wane. In this type of situation, teachers have to be persistent. They need to make it clear to parents that they will make themselves available whenever it is most convenient for the parents. Teachers have to take the onus and responsibility of making time to converse with the parents and not assume that things will happen at the next parent-teacher interview. This also involves teachers being more flexible in their availability, allowing for discussions after school, through phone calls, or even via email.

Addressing Parental Concerns and Difficulties

Encouraging parental involvement can also mean helping parents develop the skills and confidence needed to support their children's learning. This can be done through parenting classes, family literacy events, and programs such as the parent skill-building workshops. Teachers can also guide parents in creating home environments that support learning and help them understand developmentally appropriate educational practices. By demonstrating practical ways that parents can help their children succeed, teachers can empower parents and show that their involvement has a direct positive effect on their children's learning.

Parental concerns and difficulties can act as barriers to effective parent-teacher partnerships. Teachers may feel overwhelmed by the task of involving parents who seem uninterested or hard to reach. However, the educators who are most successful at involving all parents view involvement as a two-way street. They believe that regardless of a family's abilities, experiences, or time constraints, teachers can find ways to involve every parent in a positive and supportive school community. The first step in helping parents become involved is to address their specific concerns.

Building Trust and Collaboration

Another effective strategy is for teachers to be informed about the 'funds of knowledge' families possess. define this as the historically accumulated and culturally developed bodies of knowledge and skills, often embedded in everyday practices. By engaging in informal conversations with parents, where teachers seek to learn from the parents what they can about the families' history, traditions, and experiences, it is possible for teachers to see how this can be utilized in the classroom to make learning more relevant and meaningful for the child. With parents realizing that the teacher is trying to understand their child and family better, there will often be quite a shift in expectations of the teacher (often to go above and beyond just teaching the curriculum) and how support for learning can be provided into the home.

Building trust and collaboration between teachers and parents is a fundamental step to ensure the success of children's learning. Although there are no specific strategies outlined on how this should be achieved, the research emphasizes the importance of recognizing and addressing the different perspectives, beliefs, and values each group holds. Teachers and parents both have to be aware of the impact their personal experiences, culture, and society has had on forming their perspectives. By exchanging this information in an open, friendly, and informal manner, it can often reduce misinterpretations and judgment.

CHAPTER 5

Promoting Parent Engagement and Involvement

5.4. Recognizing and valuing parent contributions In schools where parents are valued and recognized, students tend to do better academically and behaviorally. Teachers and school administration can promote recognition by valuing parents' opinions and considering their ideas. This may involve regular parent-teacher group meetings and scheduled input from parents on decisions that may affect the school community. Published recognition such as newsletters and notices regarding certain parent contributions can significantly improve a parent's morale and determination to stay involved with the school.

5.3. Encouraging volunteering and participation The more parents are involved in the daily life of the school, the more they will feel part of the school community. This involvement can occur in many ways, such as decision-making, volunteering in the classroom, and participating in school events. In any case, the more the parent is involved, the more they are likely to understand the school process and be able to help their children with school-related issues.

5.2. Providing parent education and support Offering parents education to further their child's learning is advantageous for all parties involved. Parents gain greater understanding about what and how their child is learning; this in turn can bring a greater parental involvement with school and homework. Understanding that some parents may have difficulty finding time to involve themselves in learning new teaching methods and skills, teachers should try to accommodate by keeping an open communication with all parents.

5.1. Establishing a welcoming school environment To promote relations between parents and school, it is essential for the school environment to be a welcoming one, and one which the parents will feel comfortable going to. Many schools hold "Parent Nights" where parents are invited to the school to meet the teachers, and learn what the academic expectations are for their children. These nights are a great way for the parents to get a foot in the door in terms of communication, and for the teachers to express the importance of the child's learning.

Establishing a Welcoming School Environment

In order to promote school environments that are more welcoming, schools are encouraged to evaluate the manner in which they communicate with families and the message that is sent out. Welcoming environments begin with the very first contact made between the school and the home. Henderson and Mapp (2002, p. 57) recommend that schools develop more effective means of communicating with parents about school programs and their children's progress. They state that communication should be "regular, meaningful, and two-way." Smith and Vincent (1993) stress the importance of regular positive communication, particularly phone calls and notes about the positive things that are happening, rather than only during times of trouble or when strong parent involvement is needed. Finally, Epstein (2001) recommends that schools develop activities specifically aimed at reaching out to new families. These activities should help parents understand how the school works, the programs offered, and ways in which they can support their children's learning. By helping parents understand what they can expect from the school and showing them that their help is valued, schools can begin to build strong relationships with all families.

The ways in which schools welcome parents can vary widely. In some schools, the establishment of a welcoming environment is shaped by the physical appearance of the school or through the friendliness of its staff. Whatever the form, a welcoming environment promotes parent engagement and makes parents feel comfortable and confident in becoming involved in the educational process. Smith and Vincent (1993) report that parents are more likely to become involved in school activities if they perceive the atmosphere to be positive and supportive. They are also more likely to take part in school decision making. Clark (2002) states that when parents feel more comfortable about their place in the school community, they are more likely to become involved in their child's education.

Providing Parent Education and Support

Effective organisations tend to offer various educational services and support for parents to help them better understand their child's learning and developmental needs, support homework and other curriculum-linked activities at home, stay informed about their child's progress, and engage effectively with educators, administrators, and other parents. Parent education is most effective when schools and other organisations offer a series of parent education events or workshops linked to students' educational stages and provide opportunities for skill-building and to practice new skills. Topics for parent education may be generated based on parent, teacher, and administrator concerns and interests. A needs assessment of parents' interests and desired skills or knowledge may be conducted to guide the planning of events. Parents are also more apt to attend and benefit from education events when they are provided with specific information on the benefits of the event or topic chosen and targeted in advertising efforts that reach them effectively.

Encouraging Volunteering and Participation

Illinois has an increasingly diverse student population, many living in poverty with parents who have limited English proficiency or low literacy levels. Although strong parent involvement is known to increase children's academic success, these parents are less likely to be involved in their child's education. The Parent Mentor Program trains parents to serve as mentors and leaders in their schools and communities to help other parents become more involved in their child's education. This program is beneficial for all parents and has shown to increase student academic achievement. An increase in parent involvement has also been shown to have an impact on students with disabilities. Because these students are often accompanied by an aide or parent, teachers may feel uncomfortable asking them to leave the room to volunteer. By providing in-class activities specifically for these parents, K-3 parents can be encouraged to volunteer and aid those students without feeling stigma.

After parents understand the value of parent involvement and want to be involved, schools can take the next step and encourage volunteering and active participation in their child's education. Studies of parent involvement today reflect a concern for busy parents and lack of convenient and flexible ways for working and other parents to be involved. Often, programs are set up that cater to the availability and demands of teaching professionals rather than the needs and capabilities of the parents they are trying to serve. One good way to do this is to offer a variety of activities that parents can do from home. This will help to get all parents involved and create greater success in parent involvement. Teachers can have materials ready for parents to take home, and programs can be designed to make telephone calls to parents about school events and updating parents about school progress a more regular occurrence. Another program design that has been successful for creating home-based parent involvement in the state of Illinois is The Parent Mentor Program.

Recognizing and Valuing Parent Contributions

Henderson and Berla have stated that, "The most accurate predictor of student achievement is the extent to which the family is able to be involved in their child's education." Parent engagement and involvement in their child's education has been shown to have a positive effect. Despite this evidence, many parents feel unvalued, uneasy, and sometimes unwanted in their child's school. Educators and schools often fail to recognize the potential and diversity of contributions that parents can make to influence a child's success. Schulz argues that there is a bias among educators and administrators "to set the terms of engagement for parents, viewing them as recruits to serve the school rather than as advocates for their children." It is important for schools to value the wealth of knowledge that families bring, viewing them as equal partners in the education of their children. By recognizing and valuing parent contributions, schools are able to increase the level of involvement and engagement of all families. There are many ways to recognize and value parent contributions. First and foremost, it is important for teachers and administrators to have an understanding of the many cultural contexts in which families define involvement. This book has emphasized the importance of culture throughout, stressing that parents should be viewed as equal, no matter their socioeconomic or cultural upbringing. By showing understanding and appreciation of different cultures, schools are sending a positive message to all families. An example of this could be seen in a teacher adjusting conference times in order to accommodate working parents. This simple act values the contributions and time of the parents, increasing the likelihood of parent involvement.

Celebrating Successes and Achievements

As with any successful human endeavor, achieving success and continued progress in parent involvement takes hard work and commitment. Schools with long-term, comprehensive programs to promote family and community involvement will have the highest student achievement. A recent meta-analysis showed that, more than anything else a parent does, parent expectation of student success has the greatest effect size on student achievement. To bring all parents to this level of expectation will take leadership and persistence. The results, however, will be well worth the effort.

One school with a diverse ethnic population used the PTA's cultural arts program to bring parents into the school to share their cultures and heritages. The parents took pride in their children's accomplishments and became the school's strongest supporters. In a similar grassroots effort, a small group of minority parents in another school developed a shared vision of what they wanted for their children and galvanized the school community to help all minority students achieve to higher standards.

Successful collaboration brings many achievements, both small and large. Some schools have found that successful parent involvement has led to improved student behavior, higher grades and test scores, and increased enrollment in higher-level programs. Involved parents also bring about teacher success. Teachers involved with parents are more likely to stay in the teaching profession.

CHAPTER 6

Conclusion

It is reasonable and expected for a parent to have a general idea of what their child is doing with their teacher in the classroom. An effective way for a parent to stay informed is by having regular informal contact with the teacher or other school staff with opportunities for parent-teacher interaction. This can be by talking before or after school, phoning the school, or speaking to the teacher when there are school functions. A great way to keep in touch with your child's progress and their learning environment is to stay familiar with what is happening in the classroom. Try to obtain a class newsletter, school calendar, homework requirements, or a class event schedule. By staying up to date and communicating with the teacher, both parties can have a common understanding of the child's strengths, areas needing improvement, learning style, and progress.

Often unused and unappreciated, there are many resources that a school can provide for a parent to get involved in teacher and student activities. High parent involvement and successful collaboration with teachers is shown to lead to greater benefits for their children, increased professional development for teachers, and increased likelihood for continuing parent participation.

Ask your child to show you what they have to do and help sort it before they begin so you can clarify how much time you will both expect to be spent on the task. This is also a good time to ask your child if they have any assignments or projects that they need to do soon. By tracking your child's progress in school and being involved in it, you are not only furthering their academic development, you are showing that your child's schooling is a priority for you and for them. This will lead to an increased likelihood to succeed.

Parent's involvement in the child's education does not stop with choosing the school. They need to be vigilant in all school-related activities, especially those that will affect their child. Key among the ways a parent can help their child with learning is through the facilitation of homework and the tracking of progress. Parents can assist their child in many different ways to help them help themselves in homework. This includes explaining how to plan and write a piece of work, revising what they have done, or simply helping them with a difficult task. The importance here is showing an interest and a willingness to get involved, without taking control and doing the work for them. A child's learning can be improved greatly simply by knowing that what they do is important.

www.ingramcontent.com/pod-product-compliance
Lightning Source LLC
LaVergne TN
LVHW092102060526
838201LV00047B/1526